An Infusion of Violets

An Infusion of Violets

NANCY NAOMI CARLSON

LONDON NEW YORK CALCUTTA

 **Seagull Books, 2019**

© Nancy Naomi Carlson, 2019

This compilation © Seagull Books, 2019

ISBN 978 0 8574 2 645 1

British Library Cataloguing-in-Publication Data
A catalogue record for this book is available from the British Library

Typeset by Seagull Books, Calcutta, India
Printed and bound by Hyam Enterprises, Calcutta, India

For my sister, Judy Ackerman, with love . . .

contents

An Infusion of Violets

I

Sari-Covered Nights

I'm a brass-bellied Buddha's dream,
an evening of gauze, stars blue
and windswept, the quicksilver moon
tangled in the limbs of a lone banyan tree.
Oh, rub me to a blinding sheen!

I am the sitar's ragged throat, pitched
between here and when,
caught in quartertones, worlds bewitched.
Why these four arms so long unkissed?
Am I not your goddess?

My five mouths roll their uvulas,
guttural as high winds crossing desert dunes.
Is there not a stopping place for us,
adrift, two souls who speak in tongues?

Landscape with Figure in Blue

Too early for full light, yet the wrens
have been calling an hour now, mate to mate,
while within walls subdued in pale golds
as in a painting by Hopper, a neighbor's hands
calm her cat on the windowsill.

The cat, sensing a boy or man or deer
in the shared yard, tracks the dog
at the end of my leash.
The dog seems blasé, but for the twitching ear,
and ignores me, too, on the side porch

in my terry robe—a man's terry robe
with hood, blue, or what years of rinse
and spin render what was blue something less—
the robe I bought for chilled days
of late thaw when the dog must go out

and no man here for the robe,
none for the dog,
though any one of three husbands,
here and gone, might have left such a robe,
and each might disagree about who

 6

did the leaving, but not what was left:
the Japanese maple burning
orange-red at the curb;
a small dog that jumps like a deer or boy,
or man, vanishing into the early light.

Looking Back

That blessing of salt—
chlorine and sodium ions bound
like bodies in love.

A desert I held in my hands.

Once I sprinkled salt on a magpie's tail
to keep it from flying, but fooled
by its mournful, mirrored, lake-lit self,
it gathered away on a current of wind,

song hurled against a hunter's moon.

If you want a lover back, it's said,
burn salt for seven days.
If it flares into flames, you're doomed
to pick every grain out of hell when you die,

like Persephone, feeling the pull of spilled
and broken things, or Lot's wife,
still unnamed,

 8

from whose tears,
I believe—not the pillar—the Dead Sea arose,
Sodom and Gomorrah below,
so much salt a body floats away,
really no effort at all.

Translating Myself

Elle allait sur la pointe de ses pieds nus . . . et pâle, sans parler,
sérieuse, elle s'abattait contre sa poitrine, avec un long frisson.
Gustave Flaubert

Aveling's Bovary comes to Leon *barefooted,*
but Russell's Bovary tiptoes *on bare feet.*
The difference begs definition. A doubled supplication—
pieds nus losing truth in the twice translated,
like a copperhead shedding its skins.
Tell me the perfect words to bring me to you—

as if *perfect* were not petals of abstraction,
white and unknowable, but the fruit of here and now,
thick and earthy, weighing down the tongue.
Would you have me come in well-heeled pumps
or spiked heels, wobbly and drunk?
Sneakers padding the floor, laces trailing like adders?

Or stripped to essentials—flesh and bone.
But *barefooted* or on *bare feet*?
Bare feet seem too plodding, since I would be light footed
and running toward you. But would I *throw myself*
upon your breast with a long shudder, swooping
like a tern, wings beating against her own dazed reflection,

or *sink* into your arms with an equally long shudder?
No, if I were to sink, it would be into the green pool
of your eyes—more of a resurfacing,
an emergence from the long cocoon of longing.
A dipping, as a taper that grows, or a plating of gold,
or a brioche brushed golden with yolk, devoured.

Prophetess

We now drink from Miriam's cup,
the waters of Miriam's well in the wilderness.
Reconstructionist Passover Haggadah

Drink from this cup as if mine,
and though not wine,

be drunk with dance and music,
the many shapes happiness assumes:

timbrel, wind, reed.
Let me well within you

as you await desert blooms,
or lie down in me as in a sea,

and I will cleanse what is not whole,
will hold what I cannot heal.

I am no Elijah's cup
filled with what you cannot touch.

I will be yours, the lip
where rock meets spring.

Infusion: *Round III*

A coded language emerged from a morpheme sea:
Hyperplasia, exemestane, nuclear grade.
Charmed times are not evoked in threes.

Three weeks between infusions, reprised
In frayed dreams of the needle's wake.
A broken language emerges. A lymph sea

Reels with vertigo. Red blood cells retreat.
I am bald and moon-faced.
Where's the harm in threes,

Cytoxan whispers, corroding nails as it seethes
Drip by drip in recalcitrant veins.
A muted language merges with closed seas

Of blood so pale, a slight shift of disease
Could set off a swell so untamed
That evoking three times three times three

Charms may not be enough to save me.
My body knows how it will end but remains—
With or without charmed times evoked in threes—
A veiled language merging with closed seas.

Cliffs at Étretat

To paint the sea really well, you need to look
at it every hour of every day in the same place . . .
                                    Claude Monet

Monet was drawn to Normandy's beach
Whose moods eluded the probe of his brush.
Hard to fathom what moves the sea.

Starved for wine and light, bread and heat,
He came to this surf, to the lure of unholy depths.
Something about Monet's Normandy beach

Already strewn with loss—sun's nightly retreat
And a shoreline that rides out a wave—
Kept calling him back. Urge to know what moves the sea

To rise up against cliff and rock with such zeal,
Though it shatters to mist, chromatic and pure?
Metaphors drawn from Normandy's beach,

So close to the mouth of the Seine? Knees
Soaked in brine, he'd study reflections of coastal light
As it moved from the east, gilding the sea;

Stony coral stranded on reefs
Withstanding the wear of clouds and tides;
Swirl and draw of wings on Normandy's beach—
Oil rising to life from fathoms beneath the sea.

Ask Anyone

Ask anyone who's ever lived alone
How houses seem to shift when winter comes.
It's hard to settle in against the cold.

Minor sounds grow amplified: groans
From sinking eaves, surfaces that rub.
Anyone who's lived alone knows

The shape silence takes, framed by closing
Doors and intermittent furnace hum.
It's hard to settle in. Against the cold

Bedroom window, nightly rhythms unfold:
A loose screen flaps outside, a broken shutter,
And anyone who's ever lived alone

Knows anything can hide in the quiet approach—
A brush of wings or snowdrifts piling up.
It's hard to settle in against the cold

And empty sheets, the pillow that holds
the wild scent of an abandoned love.
Ask anyone who's ever lived alone—
It's hard to settle in against the cold.

Juno's Garden

Jupiter spades the earth and sows the sky
while I tend thistle, mountain laurel, sage,
and a tumbleweed fire—hearthless, undying.

Nothing lasts for long above the tree line—
not even omens, clouded and shifting shapes.
Jupiter spades the earth and sows the sky

with pigeons, centaurs, bears, and broken lyres.
Music tuned to loss descends with rain.
I tend a tumbleweed fire—artless—that cannot hide

plots where nothing grows, where I've
planted diadems, Mother's pearls, and peacock tails.
Jupiter spades the earth and sows the sky.

In this rock garden, under a layer of schist, lies
swan's down, white and tender—oh so tender—saved
from a tumbleweed fire—breathless and blind;

darts from Cupid's bow that have strayed;
Semele's heart and Lamia's eyes.
Jupiter spades the earth and sows the sky.
I tend a tumbleweed fire—heartless, unbridled.

Lagniappe

You buy a dozen beignets from a Cajun stall
in New York, and they toss the good measure into your box.
Wiping the powdered sugar from your lips
you think *lagniappe*, from the Creole
by way of Quechua—*yapay*—"to give more."

You think bus routes on Saturday nights,
you and your then-husband queued up
against a brick wall on Canal Street
amid gold-capped smiles, as you waited to leave
the French Quarter for a room you could afford.

You think hikes through swamps
teeming with fire ants, years down the road—
your second trip to the Café du Monde,
waltzing Cajun-style with your Navy Seal,
another port of call.

You think Peter, the third-time charm:
hotel suite on Bourbon Street;
jazz flooding stairwells and cramped rooms;
beer-battered, deep-fried cod with a friend
who'd lost her foot when a car jumped the curb.

On her studio shelves, a riot of ceramic roosters,
headless and glazed, and life-sized hearts—
maybe signs your marriage would end
before Peter's heart would stop too soon.

On a Line by John Crowe Ransom

Deep freeze settles in.
Skinned and boned
it gnaws at eaves
and etches leaf patterns
into plate glass.

Trees stand helpless
under its reign.
March birdsong
has died, and I
have been bedridden

for thirty-six hours.
Chills and fever,
fever and chills—
citrus-toned and mean,
they squeeze your breath,

your dreams.
Snow curdles like milk,
force-fed into gaping
holes that fill and dissolve
into birthday cake,

icing vanilla white.
I think how sleep
is like riding on ice—
no certainty
you can stop.

Subsistence of Crickets

SCHOOL COUNSELOR'S LOG

They get by on leavings—living dust
and fungi, even glue on my cardboard box.

What she would give to learn their song.

If she could, she'd be thin as a needle
threading brackish waves.
Better still, the space of a needle's eye.

Acheta domesticus—house cricket—
omen of fortune, hope, or impending rain.

Each day her eyes sink deeper into her skull.

Her bones rebel, but cannot break her will.
The gang plank creaks under her walk.

She says crickets heralded land for the crew
of Cabeza de Vaca, just as their water ran out.

She keeps one caged by her bed for luck.

Anorexia nervosa drones in her blood,
slows her heart with its kiss.

Shunning the light, it's spooked
by my presence and scatters—confusion
of spindly legs and wings.

Day XIX

X-rays run me through,
angled past my baldness, my breath
with a skim of light across my skin.
And feeling nothing and seeing less,
I invent the plight of ions—
phantom particles blasting black holes

in my culpable left breast.
The machine clucks and whirs,
blends with white dreaming Christmas

piped into this wintry scene.
A sigh could shred my heart.
More rads zipping by than a summer

of black monazite sand, dividing
all of Brazil into fractions of grays
for nineteen days in a row.

Each layer of skin reddens and weeps.
Bare breasted, tattooed and scarred,
I ride electromagnetic waves

that see through me.
Calendula can't salve my body
from rubbing against itself.

II

Selle de Veau à la Tosca

Picture braised, sliced veal loins purloined
from the bone and restored, laid over a bed
of cut pasta with truffles and cream—

did I mention the sauce Mornay?—for queen
or diva a fitting tribute, or the perfect dish
for the prelude to a tryst set, let's say,

in Rome against the ruins, or *Palazzo Farnese*, or maybe
the Tiber, sweat beading on our sunburned flesh
like rain on an apple, golden and delicious, rare

and forbidden, each bite's aftertaste
another hunger, a scene glazed like raku, hot
from the kiln—sapphire sky, white crests of a river

out of control, an overflow, an other-worldly tint—
Sant'Andrea della Valle bells tolling, veristic pitch.

Yom Kippur

Even my sins shadow themselves
these downsized days, *For the sin*
we sinned before you by acting callously . . .

I believe in the howl of a heart after it's been breached.
I believe in a belly's growl after a day's fast—
tight fist of want in a sucker punch.
I believe how our prayers, like steam ascend
then fall unanswered—ashen at dusk
as this mantis who rests on the hood of my car
as I head back to shul, her forelegs bent like a supplicant—
irony caught—motionless, and at first glance dead.

. . . And for the sin we sinned before you forcibly or willingly.

I blow on her wings and she shifts her weight—
a movement so slight, almost missed.

Forgive us the breach of positive and negative commands,
whether or not they involve an act or are known to us.

She holds her ground, the mating, the gorging.

Infusion: *Round II*

HIGH HOLY DAYS

Forgive my body its trespasses: veins
stiff-necked, pulse flailing,
platelets shipwrecked,
resisting this intravenous gift.

The thrush's song goes unsung.

Pardon my raving tongue
that slanders the kill–cure.

Forgive this desertion of hair—
even these dark lashes—
and the earth-pull of hives.

Grant these wayward cells
atonement, full of themselves,
overcome with wanderlust.

The reign of ravaged saliva has begun.

Baudelaire's Pillared Temple

Perfumes, hues, and sounds echo one another.
                                Charles Baudelaire

Nature as *pillared temple*—I'll go along,
even accept that columns speak,
though the words are mumbled, muted.

Yes to *perfumes mellow as oboes*—maybe malachite-blue?—
or perfumes depraved as horns, yellow as tamarind wood.

Crimson for Sousa's brass and shine,
and for Bessie Smith, scales ascending violet to red,
the chromatic halftones: yellow-orange, chartreuse.

Consider a red-brick church in New Orleans
that barely stands, flood line ten feet high.
A boy with a cello cracked at the bridge
stares at heat rising to stained glass boarded shut.

If I paint this scene in oils, viscous as pitch,
can I measure the cost of a blink?

To Melancholia, Mon Amour

Because I want to leave you
something beautiful, I will dye
these sheaves of silk blood red.
You'll see them billow and rise between pairs
of stage hands—Handel's *Israel in Egypt*—
parting the sea as easy as stripping a bed.

I will make of these plagues a tapestry
thick with must and the pale infusion of moon,
or, better still, a double choir—for beasts and boils,
frogs and diamonds of hail.

Let me go, and I'll rosin my bow for the whirr of flies,
or the wheels of your chariot in pursuit—
stallions black as the growing dark—
or my strings unstrung, straining like locust wings.

Glass, Glorious Glass!

AT THE RENWICK GALLERY

Let me be your molten glass, any shape
you desire: free-blown chalice; champagne flute

whose rim rings perfect "A's;" embellished coupe.
Emerald and gold-leaf Venetian, I'll stain

your lips with "Inventing Fountains of Thor,"
or glaze them red with "Ruby and Rosette."

Fill me with your fire and make me conform
to your breath, writhing in the heat but not

consumed. Make me blossom birds of paradise
or weave me wings of indigo or white—

I'll be bunting or angel drawn from the heart
of flame, rare as ancient fragments of glass

recovered near Persia. Hold me to the light
and see through me, sheer as a veiled night.

Awaking to Vivaldi's "Four Seasons"

The deer must wonder at this frosted sunrise,
salt lick iced over, each linden limb doubled
in weight, each blade of grass enclosed
in its own sheath that splinters underfoot
beneath a patchwork of Halloween leaves
gathered like souls unearthed and ambered.

He pulls her back under the quilt
and fingers the length of her sternum
as if burnishing a Chinese flute
recovered after nine thousand years,
made from the wing bone of an extinct bird.
"Music of the spheres," he whispers and plays
the sun at middle "G," then Venus,
Mercury, the elements of fire, water, and air
scaled to the end, down to the scorched earth.

My Father's Hosta

I say *yes* to the square of earth he digs up
from his Rockville yard, hosta tips newly sprung.

He's afraid they'll die, left behind,
leaves lance-shaped, folded tight

like children's hands.
They come back each June,

and he takes them wherever he moves—
from his first home in Queens

to this room with a single bed.
There may not be a garden where he's headed.

"Plant them with sedge and bine,"
my father instructs, as he nudges roots.

Knowing the ground always claims
its own, I still promise to keep them alive.

What My Father Knows

My father knows his mind is leaving,
cells fleeing a mineshaft's dark.
He remembers the color of Laddie's coat—
first of a long line of dogs—but forgets the shade
of my mother's eyes when she leaves the room.

How long before he forgets her face
and the fire of her auburn hair?

Each night she pours him dragon brew
to head off the gathering chill,
chides him when he spills a drop—
from highest mountains come finest teas.

She invents a tale of an emperor—K'ang Ha—
who seduces a red-haired beauty beneath a gingko tree.
A pot of water simmered nearby.
As she finger-combed her shimmering hair,
three strands broke free to ride the wind
into the steaming brew—
now transformed into liquid amber, jasmine-oiled—
a dynasty of song.

My father inhales her words.

Gladys

FOR MY MOTHER

She calls them by their Latin names—
Ageratum, whiteweed,
Brachycome iberidifolia, Swan River daisy—
a foreign tongue to me.

For any lapse, she keeps a pocket guide nearby.
She says they wear their feelings on their leaves.

She points to one with pink blossoms, valentine-shaped,
strung along a showy raceme.

Dicentra spectabilis, Venus's car, bleeding heart.

Under her care, none dare wilt,
though her own heart stumbles and fails,
blooms sweet arrhythmias, atrial flutters—

now metered beats implanted in her chest.

I help her weed and water infant shoots:
hawthorn to balance her blood's pH;
lemon balm for a daughter's sleep.

She barely recalls the night her heart gave out—
mosaic of dark, tunnel of watery light,
a voice in Yiddish, calling . . .

Her favorite—*Gladiolus carneus*, sword lily,
painted lady—I name *Gladys* for short.

She says plants reach for the sun, always,
but even dazzled, will not let go.

Memory Care

FOR MY FATHER

Each day looks the same in the room of his mind
with its shrinking walls and single bed of stone.
In an endless loop, he asks for the day and time.

He tries to lasso my words to write
them down, but they dissolve into skywriter smoke.
Each day looks the same. In the room of his mind

where theorems and proofs were once enshrined,
he's trapped in a tangle of black holes.
In an endless loop he asks for the day and time

to tether himself to my mother's side.
He begs to go home to watch his hosta grow.
Each day looks the same in the room of his mind,

though I bear different gifts: hyssop sprigs to line
his bed, and a string quartet played on an iPhone
in an endless loop. He asks for the day and time.

No one knows he'll die next Sunday night
in a morphine cloud, but he senses the end is close.
Each day looks the same in the room of his mind.
In an endless loop, he asks for the day. And time.

Wolf Moon

This moon seeps through, leaves
no clue where it's going or where it's been,
poker-faced through five decades of fall.

It holds me fast in its orange tint,
hints new love, the kind that staves off
dark spaces that multiply by night—

teak chairs in the breakfast nook,
empty rooms with unplugged clocks,
time stopped on old soccer trophies,

wide-eyed, open-armed plush,
and layered in bottom drawers like mulch,
magazines that once mattered to my son.

These rooms fill and expand with the past.
Its presence gleams in this world
with feral eyes. It paws past papered walls,

skulks by mirrors, scarred and lined,
past unlit candles in cut glass rings
that wait to burn in someone's name.

And in the dust, shades fainter
than any howl, a cricket's thrill—
as if it alone outlasts the cold.

Cutting the Light

She cuts so she can bleed.
She says pain is only skin-deep.
Razor blades cut open the light.

Sometimes it's an offending thigh
Or wrist, though she doesn't want to die.
She cuts so she can feel

Fetal moons and painted seas
Rise from flesh and blood, released.
Razor blades reflect the light,

As do pins, broken glass, and knives.
She says they call to her each night.
She cuts so she can see

If the blood against her blade is real.
How much deeper is too deep?
Razor blades let in the light.

Her scars are proof that she survives.
How can I take away this rite?
She cuts so she can heal.
Razor blades become the light.

Sighting for Life

Early spring and the wrens croon as if in full
season, though we've only seen one honeybee

poised on the edge of the hyacinth's frill
near where we threw the pumpkin last Halloween.

No trace is left of its decomposed grin,
as if its soul had flown once the crows

gathered in a black shudder had had their fill.
A pair of geese strut near the lake to comb

the shore for crumbs. "They mate for life," I say,
"uncommon in the order of man or birds."

Awkward in their push and pull of gait,
wing and glide their usual means, the first

dives into the water; the other follows suit,
the surface renewed after the scrawl of two's.

What Adam Knows

Early morning, and he is moved by the peony heads,
bowed by what he calls grace—
ground strewn with tissue-pink shreds,
long stems curved like Eve's back when she bends
in dance, her hair waving thick as waterfalls,
and even now, in sleep, veiling her face.
He knows the feel of her skin, her scent an outpour,
honeyed and pure,
the give and take of hands over time
as he tracks each sunrise that highlights her hair,
and measures days by the growth of vinca vines.
He has no name for absence of breath as he feels
her breathe, though wind is air for want of words,
and nightfall belongs to her—ceding light, an evening.

III

Infusion of Violets

His blood harbors pirates,
bandanas red as the one that hides
sixteen stitches engraved in his scalp—

red as the matador print on my door.

His T-cells call to me each night, glowing . . .

Five-pointed stars tattooed on his lower calf
emerge from one pant leg rolled.

*I follow their breathless trail, find him
face up in moon-slicked grass,
forming the sign of the Cross.*

Crips, Bloods, a twelve-gauge wrench,
Elisa's lips sneaking behind every wall.

*Violets fill his mouth, the cavity of his chest,
replace the marrow in his bones.*

His blood caresses each cell it feeds—

prayer rising, thunders in our ears.

*I try to gather him up in my arms, but he breaks apart
like porcelain, a sugar skull.*

Glazunov's Azaleas

LOIRE VALLEY, 1889

On a barge drifting past Chaumont—
 metaphor drawn from catgut, reed, and brass—
he brings out reflections
 of polished wood caught in dreamy *idylls*.
From vodka spills a barrage of notes
 to stave off a dry spell; symphonic poems
emerge from river, forest and rain.
 Gone, "Cortèges solennels" of St. Petersburg,
spires rising in endless gray,
 and the suite of *S-A-C-H-A*—diminutive name—
a succession of czars
 replaced by the wash of spring engulfing the shore—
castles and vineyards ringed
 with milkweed's purple clusters, buttercups
dotting fields, and dandelion globes
 gone to seed, to air, to a place where wishes live
after they are named. And these flame azaleas—
 parched soil beauties from Greek roots: *azaleos*
meaning "dry"—flood orange-red and chaste,
 the way fire blooms from two rubbed sticks,
or a sheaf of staved paper fills with sound.

Complications of the Heart

I've heard that hearts are not just simple pumps,
but storage sites of energy—rows

of twitching desires, secret romps
muffled in its four-chambered folds.

Each part carries weight—a string quartet
whose practiced rhythms fit the everyday—

and should a section fail or skip a beat
technology can shock the whole awake.

But still no surgery to transplant love,
uprooting it intact to needed space

when one mate loves too little, one too much—
asymmetry that flusters the hearts' pace.

If balance over time won't self-correct,
demand cuts off supply and hearts defect.

The Gift

I made this panel myself.
If you are reading it I am dead . . .
   Duane Kearns Puryear, AIDS Memorial Quilt

The light leaves early these days—
late fall—and soon night and day will be
the same. Only weeks ago, the trees
had not turned, but in a flash a man can go gray.

I'm banking on a three-by-six-foot plot
of cloth to save me, my name stitched in red.

I push the needle in and out, and the thread
strains to rise, pulled back by the knotted
weight of where it's been, each gathered hour.

A certain softness eases into each edge
smoothed down by the practiced needle's tread.

The comfort of having learned to live without
fades each loss into a well-worn theme—
yet as slow to resolve as my thimbled need.

Totem Eyes

Don't trust a sky where every day means rain.
Take hold of what erodes, might wash away.
Totem eyes reflect what can't be seen.

Seagull swagger threads a sinking design
On hulls and masts that claim Vancouver Bay.
Don't trust a sky where every day means rain

Against the eaves. I could say *harbor*, mean
Your waiting arms. King salmon, hawk, or whale—
Totem eyes reflect what can't be seen.

Reel me in from winter's cold domain—
Risk of drift from opposite coasts the same.
Don't trust a sky. Where every day means rain,

The world ends at your own horizon's plane—
You only see what lies behind your gaze.
Totem eyes reflect what can't be seen

And totem mouths don't open to the sun
With news of where the moon each night has strayed.
Don't trust a sky where every day means rain.
Totem eyes reflect what can't be seen.

Saint-Pierre, Martinique

A fire seethes deep in Pelée's core,
Though flumes of steam no longer wreathe its dome.
Shades are drawn closed behind high walls.

Two lifetimes ago: the Church of the Fort
Razed by a dense black cloud that glowed
From the fire seething deep in Pelée's core.

Ascension Day, and everyone lost—
No difference if mainland French or Creole.
Shades of the dead are still drawn to these walls,

Red-tiled roofs, and voodoo shores.
Steps of charred stone lead down Hell's Road.
A fire seethes deep in Pelée's core,

In hearths of the living, behind cottage doors
On Rise-to-Heaven Street, on mountain slopes.
When shades of sunset mauve high walls,

Dark feet, white feet, quadroon feet walk
To smoky cafes for rounds of rhum agricole
To ignite a fire deep in the core—
Before shades of skin draw them back to high walls.

Eve Uncovers Her Text

One of those endless days when the sun seems fixed
mid-arc, unblinking as a cat's eye. Cloudless blue,
and no horizon to separate earth from sky.
Pure azure, she muses, in love with a text
threaded with what cannot be touched,
the words hers—not sprung from some man
or some God-given sea of sounds, one-celled
forms that grow and divide as if by free will.

Not that she'd ever leave, but sometimes she dreams
she can see beyond the garden wall,
filled with her own human nature—
maybe free as the purple flowers
that dot the hills, able to know if light falls
as bright on the other side, or if nights
are still the color of coal, filled with the lull of sleep.

What she would give for one restless night,
a pulse on fire, perhaps fueled by tea,
mango leaves leaving their scrawl in the bottom of the cup—
you must know, you must know—or shaped
like a two-headed snake, tongues speaking in different keys,

one spun from sermons and the Word,
the other bent on spreading tales, bending truths—
she squeezing berries from the juniper shrub growing wild
near the gate, blue juice anointing her hands, her mouth,
her words a permanent stain on the dried papyrus sheaf.

Forever Eve

Forever falling as in a dream, she favors colors,
like flavors, sapid and rising, free as maples that root
in cracks between rocks, in flower beds.

First yellow, awakening, fusion and birth—
marsh flower, self-sown poppy, yellow of tiger's eyes
with fried marble stare, owl eyes swiveling in sleep,

sky cerulean, porcelain smooth, breathless
as baby's breath, as columbine, flocks of doves
hovering like clouds, white as Canterbury bells.

Falling past red-tinged sunsets, blood red,
she's languid in summer heat, its laboring heart,
the garden sun-dappled and overripe, and still the need

to name what cannot be contained—the fevered blush
of standing cypress, strawflowers, Indian pinks
with serrated petals, as if cut by pinking shears,

sweet william with its clove-like scent.
And still the falling, the first fall leaving her in awe—
a bounty of pear trees christened in French,

and the glory of apples with flowered skin,
Rome beauties her most prized. She revels in the flare
of leafage, makes leaf masks shaped like faces of birds,

and mourns the fallen, piled in uneven rows.
And still the blooming of sun each day, like goldenrod,
and the coming of moon, certain as rain.

Fabled Fruit

Who could fault Eve's right to know—
her sin-filled heart exposed,
grounded day after day by the same sweet earth?

How to resist a flawless skin,
so impurely pure?
No Snow White, would I still have reached

for the crimson side, my reflection cast raw
in its shine, forsake my faith for a taste
of what I didn't own?

Maybe a lick, or would I have spit out the first
breached mouthful, wiping the juice from my lips
with a guilty hand?

Some say figs were Eve's downfall,
phallic and hidden beneath luxurious leaves,
or maybe pomegranates, thick with caverns of seeds,

but I'll stick with the fruit that led to the Trojan War—
the apple of gold, symbol of greed,
thrown "to the fairest" to seed discord.

In the end, used to having my way,
I'd have Adam take the first bite,
just as Lot let his wife look back first.

Shoring Up the Heart

New Year's Eve resolves to New Year's Day,
while pizza oils the doubled cardboard lid.
Champagne goes flat and party toys deflate.
An old year still unsettled and now this
new one heaps on like snow over layers of ice,
and we go on, as if on sure ground.
Today the yearly jump-start of your life—
you'll wade into the frigid bay and douse
yourself chest-deep, the chill of risk by degrees;
a slip below could mean the heart arrests.
You numb up so quickly, you don't feel
the chill to the bone—just weightlessness.
I'll wait with the lookers-on along the shore
until the air and I can make you warm.

Writing the Dark

Not for me, last night, my latticed window,
nor was I huddled with a lover on my deck
as winter engraved itself on the moon's
copper face. I did not see the Earth
erase the sun from the sky's bauble of moon—
rarest display on this shortest day of the year.
I would have to outlive the longest-lived
by fifty years to have a chance
to miss again this cosmic drama,
just as years ago I'd sacrificed the epic tide
of Mont-Saint-Michel, the abbey conceived
though a hole in the bishop's skull, burned there
by the pointing finger of Archangel Michael,
who gave the pious ecstatic visions
but chose to leave undisturbed my urge for sleep,
letting other-worldly miracles have their dance
while I tossed and spun in the here and now.

If You Build It

She built a sunroom to bank the honeyed light,
but by nightfall, not a drop was saved.
Patience, she prayed, room drained
even of moon. The smell of new paint
ached the lungs. She had put her faith
into star-crossed words—
cadmium lemon, corn silk, goldenrod pale—
and the hubris of human floors,
when a simple sound would do—
as in a song without words—
Rachmaninoff's "Vocalise"—instinct blooming in *oo's*—
or a river's lap and purl
surrounding a basket woven from twigs, baby asleep,
hidden from sight but buoyed by a pattern of reeds.

IV

Miriam at the Waterside

At first a leaf the water catches like the wind,
blue Nile, white Nile, and overhead flocks of thrush.
A raft of twigs and leaves, bound tight by weeds,

unbound again by soft and lazy ripples
smaller than a newborn's hands.
In the rush of wings, a shudder weaves the sky,

basket of reeds, nest of grass, blanket blue as Egypt,
infant lulled by flow and lilt of current, bulrush, purl.
Miriam's song, *weave the waters, weave the reeds,*

from darkness will come light, until drifting out of range.
A sea of reeds, a timbrel in hand, and tallith fingers
fringe the skirts and robes, eddying around bare ankles—

sing a new song, sing a song composed of salt and waves—
whatever fits an open mouth, an open palm.
Miriam sings the water into stream, the stream to river,

the river to sea, song and sea rising after heavy rain—
how they hold what must be held until they overflow—
how sorrow holds its joy and holds it once again.

Sing manna, sing *mayim*, sing Miriam—
no clepsydra measuring the wilderness—
sing waterfowl, water milfoil, waterbucks,

water's petals above and below the lily's stems
fed on what resides unseen below.
I am the shaft of light that mines your eyes.

I am the line between waking and sleep.
I am the line unthreaded in its thinning pulse
that pulls you from your dreams.

Elegy in White

I know the balm of white pine
    to stave off despair that rides currents of air
like a hawk. I am singing
    burn any clippings of nails
lest they fall into enemy hands,
    or stow them away in a crack in the wall.
I have built a stone of sacred stones.
    My baby's been dead
for over three decades, and still
    I know no dream charm to stop the rain
that fills the rivers and creeks
    and soaks the low-lying earth.
How long can my levee hold?
    I see color in whiteness,
in drops of rain that coat the crested ferns.
    I did not save his baby teeth,
nor hide them in hollows of trees,
    safe from the light of moon or sun.
Birds never wove a nest of his hair.
    I am wrapping the pearl of my grief
in a plantain leaf to cast
    adrift in the nearest canal.

Shady Grove

My fortune was told in tea leaves scattered like ash
in a gold-trimmed cup four decades ago,

but I don't remember more than the porcelain's spades
and crescent moons, a pair of geese, a bush apple tree

with a snake's open mouth—so there must have been
a snake as well—which seemed fortune enough, for then,

and perhaps for now, riding the train from Forest Glen
to Shady Grove, the end of the line, and looping back

for no reason at all, except, maybe, the sound of my own
breathing to soothe myself to sleep, strangers' bodies

pressed into mine. Women in business clothes, like the ones
I used to wear, seep in and out of underground shadows.

Voices collect like confessions of thousands of students.
Stations pass like seasons, and through my mouth,

breathe the air, drink the drink, taste the fruit—
the Thoreau on yesterday's tea bag of shapeless leaves,

counsel culled from years of daydreams
counting rings on stumps of trees.

Lake Waubeeka

DANBURY, CONNECTICUT

The lake is not what I most remember,
    opaque between water lilies whose stems
would tug at the oars my father dipped
    into surface glaze, stirring up algae and flies—
nor the outcrop of rock, my mother standing watch
    as our boat sprang leaks on its way from the shore—
but the mountain itself enclosing the lake,
    a presence, an embrace that made our Studebaker's engine
strain in different keys as gears were meshed,
    so even, eyes shut, I could guess how close we were
to the top. While my father hammered his chisel
    into the same stone on which our summer house was built,
I'd chip away mica found in the woods,
    or strip sassafras bark with my nails, then chew
its fragrant pulp. Or pull Queen Anne's lace
    by the roots, just for its carrot smell, balance
on fallen trees and tunnel through hulls,
    singing, or magnify sun on a single brown leaf.

Intravenous Lines

Nothing better to do than watch
each drop of Cytoxan shimmy

down a see-through tube
to anoint the chosen vein.

You could turn to the window's maple,
smoldering in autumn sun,

to catch the precise nanosecond
when leaf detaches from limb—

stare down a likely candidate,
curled and tinged with brown.

A nudge from the wind
might encourage the scene along,

but even then, if the angle of light
isn't just so, you'd miss

the shadow of falling leaf many yards
beyond the trunk, hitting asphalt

and racing toward its embodied self.
When leaf touches ground,

does its shadow ascend?
In these shortened days of fall,

I look for signs of renewal.
Look how the sun flares

bonfire orange and gold
as it clings to the west. Listen!

Can you still hear the freight train's
burst of horn displacing the air,

after the last boxcar
slinks behind the furthest hill?

Do only laws of physics apply?
In old movie frames, I see my mother's

young face, gardenia-pale
against dark curls. She is waving,

climbing terraced steps to a lake.
I reverse the reel at will,

my mother backing down
the stairs, then floating up again.

White Pine

Not mine, but the one dwarfed
by Gothic vaults of Elderdice Hall,
barely observed in the rush
to lecterns, interns and chalk

of my second career, until needles,
color of rust, bedecked my path,
and pine cones dotted the lawn,
seemingly fallen overnight,
like some early winter snows.

I picked one up—wooden petals closed
tight, except for three rows flaring out
from the base with thorns—a prop
I would use for my students:

tight-lipped counselee, trust slow to bloom,
stages of grief as painful as pulling out thorns.

Next day's shock: the pine cone had opened,
as if infused with something to make it more
than itself, to become itself more fully,
in a form more enduring, more endearing—
a kind of empathy I could hold.

Infusion: Round IV

A newness each day
  of this final cycle,
    despite the ones before,
      inscribed in a ledger book.

I am singing
  a children's round
    I never know when
      will end. Each hour side-

tracked, as taxol
  riffs in my blood,
    crescendos then dies,
      giving rise to legions

of lesions in mouth
  and lining of gut
    transposing itself.
      I am baby-bald. I am

all over smooth
  and buffed, and
    the blush of pristine
      skin makes me almost forget

the curtained
  ridges on nails,
    like arsenic's tracks,
      and bruises that bloom

and spread
  in muted tones
    wherever they fall—
      on parts gone numb—

and panic
  in cut-time,
    arriving by
      Day Eighteen

despite favorable
  odds for a "cure"
    of which I can only be sure
      when I die of something else.

Circadian Rhythms

Bindweed blooms at 5 a.m.,

but not in time to hear the wren

rustle through chicory—

closes by noon, unlike hawkweed,

open at six, but graces

the walk until dusk.

Each day the same,

you could almost keep

time, like Linnaeus's flower clock.

My baby was sand spurrey,

smooth cat's ear, day-lily,

shy in coming,

lasted ten hours.

He was sown into my dreams.

Reseeding each birthday year,

thirty-five years gone,

he is bristly ox tongue,

Iceland poppy, blue sowthistle,

perennial.

Acknowledgments

I would like to express my gratitude to the editors of the following publications in which these poems, sometimes in earlier versions, first appeared:

Atlanta Review: "Totem Eyes"
Bellevue Literary Review: "To Melancholia, Mon Amour"
Bethesda Magazine: "My Father's Hosta"
Blue Lyra Review: "If You Build It"
Chautauqua Literary Journal: "Cutting the Light"
The Cincinnati Review: "Intravenous Lines"
Colorado Review: "On a Line by John Crowe Ransom"
ForPoetry.com: "Sari-Covered Nights"
The Georgia Review: "Infusion: Round III," "Memory Care"
Ilanot Review: "Shady Grove"
Iron Horse Literary Review: "What Adam Knows"
Journal of the American Medical Association: "Gladys"
Little Patuxent Review: "Landscape with Figure in Blue"
The Missouri Review Online: "Lake Waubeeka"
Notre Dame Review: "Infusion of Violets," "Yom Kippur"
On the Seawall: "Infusion: Round IV"
Passages North: "Miriam at the Waterside"
Poems & Plays: "Fabled Fruit"
Poet Lore: "Prophetess"
Poetry Magazine: "Complications of the Heart"
Prairie Schooner: "The Gift," "Shoring Up the Heart," and "Sighting for Life"

Puerto del Sol: "Translating Myself"
Shenandoah: "Baudelaire's Pillared Temple," "Forever Eve," "Glazunov's Azaleas," "Juno's Garden," "Looking Back," "Selle de Veau à la Tosca," "Subsistence of Crickets" and "What My Father Knows"
The Sligo Journal: "Circadian Rhythms" and "Lagniappe"
Southern Humanities Review: "Ask Anyone" and "Glass! Glorious Glass!"
The Southern Review: "Wolf Moon"
The Texas Review: "Awaking to Vivaldi's 'Four Seasons'"

"Intravenous Lines" was republished on *Academy of American Poets* (www.poets.org).

*

Some of these poems have also appeared in *Complications of the Heart* (Texas Review Press, 2003) and *Imperfect Seal of Lips* (Poems & Plays, 2005).

*

I am incredibly thankful to Jeffrey Levine for shepherding these poems into existence over the past eighteen years, as well as to Stanley Plumly, for his spot-on critique. I am also grateful to Barri Armitage, Tina Daub, Brandel France de Bravo, Roger Greenwald, Lola Haskins, Catherine Kellogg, Ted Miller, Carol Quinn, Jeneva Stone, and Marcela Sulak for their encouragement and edits. Finally, I am deeply indebted to the Seagull team: Naveen Kishore for his faith in my work, and for bringing me to India; Sunandini Banerjee for the gorgeous cover design, and Sayoni Ghosh for her brilliant editing.